D1576518

Newport (Gwent)

in old picture postcards

by
David Jones

European Library – Zaltbommel/Netherlands

The author wishes to gratefully acknowledge the assistance of the following:
Mrs. L. Baker, Mr. A. Baldwin, Mrs. I. ter Beek, Mrs. G. Christopher, Mr. E. Coqueral, Mrs. P. Davies, Br. J. Furlong, Miss D. Inker, Mrs. A.C. Jones, Mr. and Mrs. D. Netherway, Mrs. J. Parker, Mr. and Mrs. W. Ridout, Mr. R. Sykes, Mrs. O. Wainwright and Mr. R.K. Williams.

With special thanks due to: Mr. V. Alder.

GB ISBN 90 288 5125 9 / CIP

© 1990 European Library – Zaltbommel/Netherlands

No part of this book may be reproduced in any form, by print, photoprint, microfilm or any other means, without written permission from the publisher.

Dedicated to my mother

Cyflwynedig i fy mam

INTRODUCTION

Newport it seems has always been a town of change. From *Nova Porta* AD 918-1130, little more than a fishing village to the small castled town of *Novus Burgus* or *Castell Newydd* 1130-1585. From the market town of 1585 when it appears it first received its present designation of Newport, to the period of growth and prosperity 1792-1900, when the population of the town rose from around 1,000 to over 67,000.

Such periods of change have been chronicled down the centuries, with wildly differing descriptions of the town. John Leland's sixteenth century comment *A town in decay* for instance contrasts with James Matthews early twentieth century observation... *one hundred years of Newport History during the nineteenth century shows what marvellous progress has been accomplished in that space of time, testifying to the active, energetic and persistant enterprise of its public men, who had practically created a New Town on the banks of the Usk.*

The foundations for a remarkable transformation in the fortunes of the town were laid with the commencement of the construction of the Monmouthshire Canal in 1792. Coal and iron cargoes carried along its length to Newport for shipment to worldwide destinations increased annually and in 1845 amounted to 816,905 tons. Such trade saw a rapid expansion in the town, which is perhaps best illustrated by the fact that in 1851 both its 19,323 population and 2,908 dwellings outnumbered that of nearby Cardiff. Continued growth of the town in the nineteenth century was sustained by a marked increase in cargo handled at the Docks. In 1843, the number of vessels using the port was 148 yet within little over a quarter of a century this number had risen to 1,380. Newport's rapid progression from a position of comparative insignificance to one of commercial importance was then perhaps unparalleled by any town in Britain.

Soon the wealth created by such rapid growth became evident in the development of the town itself. Almost overnight the townscape was transformed with the erection of countless grand new edifices. On one day alone in 1882 the citizens of Newport were able to celebrate the opening of a new library, hospital ward, public park and highway. The latter years of the nineteenth century saw continued industrial growth in the town which led to S.D. Williams to comment in 1892: ...*in the immediate neighbourhood of Newport the county swarms with every evidence of great industrial activity.*

Such growth which has been maintained into the present century has sadly not been without cost. An indecent haste for change and a lack of consideration for preservation have seen the disappearance of architecturally pleasing façades of instantly recognisable landmarks such as the Town Hall, Corn Exchange, Lyceum and others too numerous to mention.

So great has the pace of unrelentless redevelopment been that even during the last two decades the transformation in the town is such that an exile returning to his town of birth would be hard pressed to find his way around the Newport of today. This perhaps underlines the importance of photography in providing an invaluable record of times gone by. It is the sincere hope that the following photographs will in some small measure make a contribution to that record.

1. The Newport coat of arms has an interesting history which dates back to the fourteenth century. In 1858, Newport Council made efforts to confirm the exact design of the Borough Arms and discovered that officially Newport did in fact not possess any formal coat of arms. It was further revealed that the corporate seal which had been used in the town for centuries bore the shield of the Stafford family, who were Earls and Dukes of Buckingham and Lords of the Manor of Newport during the fourteenth and fifteenth centuries. The Newport seal, however, differed by having a reversed chevron, a design unknown in heraldry. In 1929, moves were made to seek official recognition for the arms depicting a winged cherub over a gold shield charged with the reverse red chevron. On 7th May 1958 approval was granted for the addition of winged sea lion and dragon supporters to the arms. The motto *Terra Marique* means 'By Land and Sea'.

2. Principal town of the county of Gwent formerly known as Monmouthshire, Newport's Welsh pedigree is undoubted. Following the Act of Union 1536 Monmouthshire was formed from land west of Offa's Dyke − *in the country of Wales*. Later confusion regarding the county's Welsh status appears to have occurred due to it being taken under the jurisdiction of the Oxford circuit, simply for the sake of convenience. The Welsh language has had a chequered history in the county and it is perhaps remarkable that it has survived at all. Undoubtedly commercial development hastened anglicisation and by the 1970's only two per cent of the people in the county spoke Welsh. Since then, though there has been a revival in the fortunes of the language in Gwent, no doubt assisted by the staging of The Royal Welsh National Eisteddfod at Newport in 1988.

3. An early nineteenth century view of Newport from Fairoak Hill, Christchurch, by James Flewitt Mullock. Around this time Newport had only one main street which stretched from the castle to St. Woolos Church. The population of the town then was only around 1,000 people.

OLD NEWPORT IN 1866

J F MULLOCK
SEE ON

4. Newport 1866. Within half a century the population of the town had grown to over 20,000. The stone bridge was built in 1800 and the rail bridge featured in the foreground in 1848. The latter was destroyed by fire on 31st May 1848 whilst under construction. The fire which resulted in the centre arch becoming engulfed in flames and finally crashing into the river was reported as being caused by one of the workmen using a bolt that had been overheated.

THE HOUSE IN WHICH JOHN FROST, THE CHARTIST, LEADER, WAS BORN, THOMAS ST; NEWPORT, MON.

5. Newport's most famous son John Frost was born on 25th May 1784 in the Royal Oak Inn, Thomas Street. After serving an apprenticeship with a Cardiff tailor he opened a drapery business in Mill Street in 1811. Soon the respected middle class businessman became engrossed in radical politics and in 1822 was jailed. This failed to temper his passion for working class rights and with the popular support of the people of the town he became Mayor of Newport in 1836. Three years later, on Monday 4th November 1839, he was one of the leaders of the Chartist march to Newport.

6. The Westgate Hotel 1860, when the exterior was much the same as it was at the time of the Chartist attack of 1839. Then, Chartist marchers gathered outside the hotel and shouted for the release of fellow Chartists imprisoned in the cellars. A shot rang out and thirty soldiers concealed in the hotel opened fire on the crowd outside, killing twenty-two Chartists. John Frost and his fellow leaders were arrested and sentenced to be hanged and quartered, although this was later commuted to transportation for life. In 1854 Frost was pardoned and returned to Newport a hero. He died at Stapleton, Bristol, on 28th July 1877 at the age of 93.

7. The earliest mention of a town bridge over the Usk at Newport appears to be from around the twelfth century. Prior to the erection of this timber structure the only way to cross was probably to ford the river at low tide. The first stone bridge of five arches was built in 1800 at a cost of £10,165 by David Edwards, son of the builder of the famous single-arched bridge at Pontypridd. On the left is the Bridge Hotel, later the site of the Shaftesbury Café and in the far distance the 'Old Dip'.

Clarence Bridge, Newport, Mon.

8. Formerly known as Clarence Bridge, a census taken at the Town Bridge on 23rd December 1864 revealed heavy use by Newport citizens. During the hours 7am-7pm 444 wagons and carts, 109 carriages and gigs, 98 saddle horses, 74 handcarts, 20 asses and carts and 7 cattle were recorded. In addition no less than 3,725 foot passengers were counted.

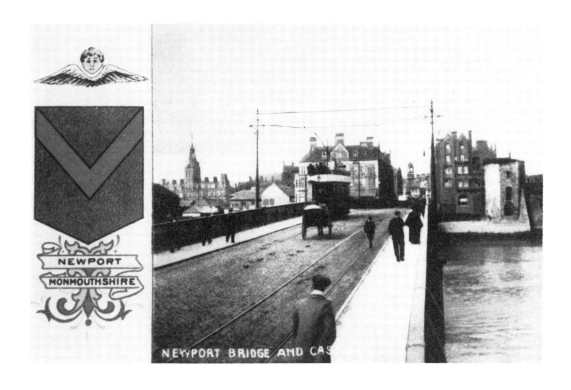

NEWPORT BRIDGE AND CAS...

9. Newport Bridge and Castle about 1910. In the distant left the market, immediate left the Shaftesbury Café, which in 1915 became Jay's Furnishing Stores. In the centre can be seen the Corn Exchange and behind the Castle, the Shaftesbury Hotel.

10. Town Bridge about 1924. On the right a temporary additional bridge erected at a cost of £40,000 following a recommendation in a Borough engineers report of 1920. The temporary structure which originally spanned the River Thames at Southwark Bridge was opened at Newport on 22nd November 1922 and remained in place until 1927.

11. Two Newport Bridges. The Town Bridge and Railway Bridge. The latter carries the advertisement 'Furnish at Ganes, 161-162 Commercial Street, Cheapest and Best'. In the far distance can be seen Lovells confectionery factory, Crindau.

NEW BRIDGE OVER RIVER USK, NEWPORT, MON.

12. New Bridge over the River Usk 1927. Construction of the present bridge designed by Mott, Hay & Anderson of London commenced on 10th June 1924. The contractors were Sir William Arrol & Company and the cost of completion including the provision of the temporary bridge was £226,744. This figure did not include the cost of purchase of the Shaftesbury Hotel, Castle Yard and other buildings which amounted to an additional £59,525.

13. The bridge was officially opened on 22nd June 1927 by Colonel the Right Honourable Wilfred William Ashley M.P., Minister of Transport. Formally declaring the bridge open 'for use of the King's subjects forever' he cut a white tape at the town end and then repeated the ceremony at the Maindee end.

14. The landing stage on the River Usk 1908. Around this time paddle steamers were a regular feature in the town reaches of the Usk. Weston and Clevedon were the favourite destinations for Newport daytrippers.

15. Campbell's pleasure steamer S.S. 'Glenavon' at the landing stage on the east bank about 1912. In the centre can be seen the dome of the new Technical College and the junction of Rodney Road and St. Vincent Road. On the left Davies Brothers – DeeBee builders merchants.

Newport, Mon., Bridge & Castle.

16. Built on a sandstone bluff, the origins of Newport Castle date back to the twelfth century, when a wooden structure was established which was later replaced with a stone fortification. Over the next five centuries the castle was rebuilt a number of times after being the scene of much conflict including sieges by Owain Glyndwr in 1402 and Oliver Cromwell in 1648. It was at the hands of Cromwell's men that the castle was finally damaged beyond repair.

17. Legend has it that Cromwell's men were aided by a traitor who revealed a secret underground passage to the castle and stories circulated that part of such a tunnel were discovered when excavations for the Monmouthshire Canal were undertaken in the latter part of the eighteenth century. A ghost, a bearded figure with piercing eyes, possibly the traitor who was later found hanged, is still said to haunt the ruins.

18. In the early nineteenth century the castle bailey was used as a tannery and the South Tower as a nail factory. 1828 saw the conversion of the North Tower into a brewery, which continued to trade there for the next seventy years. At the end of the last century Lord Tredegar presented the castle to the town with the proviso that 'the remains should be preserved and historic portion restored'. Finally, in 1930 the castle was taken into the care of the Ministry of Works.

19. Looking towards Clarence Place from the Old Green 1912. On the left Griffiths & Sons and the Shaftesbury Hotel and in the distance the familiar dome of the new Technical College which was completed in 1910. The sign on the far right points the way to E. Hill's Shoeing and General Forge.

20. High Street about 1929. Familiar High Street names of Bannister & Thatcher, Lovells and the Old Green Hotel, all swept away with development of the Old Green interchange. On the far right is the King's Head Hotel, which was rebuilt in 1900.

HIGH STREET.

NEWPORT.

1570

21. High Street around the turn of the century. On the left is the now demolished Corn Exchange, first opened on 4th September 1878. Erected on the site of the once famous 'Pyes Shop' the 'Tredegar Memorial Corn Exchange' as it was formally known was built by public subscription in memory of Lord Tredegar.

22. A new Post Office was opened in High Street on Thursday 18th July 1907 by His Majesty's Postmaster General, the Right Honourable Sydney Charles Buxton M.P. Following the opening a celebratory supper was held at the Drill Hall, Stow Hill. Music was provided by the Post Office Band.

Newport, New Post Office & Savoy Hotel

23. Within less than a decade Newport's new Post Office was considered too small and in 1914 the adjoining and also newly built Savoy Hotel and Silver Grill were acquired for later expansion.

24. Looking down High Street from Station Approach. To the left, the timber-framed, Tudor style Murenger House, in the centre Lovells café and to the left the entrance to Newport Arcade.

25. Sons of Newport off to war. New recruits pass the Murenger House in High Street enroute to Newport Station and Kitchener's Army, on 31st August 1914. The way is led by the Newport Tramway Band.

26. Looking up High Street from Westgate Square. High Street was originally much narrower but considerably widened during the 1880's. On the left is the National Provincial Bank of England, now the National Westminster Bank. On the left is the Scottish Temperance Life Assurance Company, today known as Aspen ladies fashion shop.

High Street, Newport, Mon.

27. High Street about 1906. The number 36 tram makes its way along a busy High Street. On the right Olivers shoe shop, on the left Kibbler family butcher and a surgeon dentist offering painless extraction of aching teeth.

28. High Street at night 1913. Often in an effort to increase sales, postcard manufacturers would produce
a night shot by adapting an existing photograph to
produce a more dramatic effect.

29. Prior to the 1800's the area now known as Bridge Street was an expanse of agricultural land known as Six Acres Field. Before development of the area could commence, consideration had to be given to the demolition of a barn on the site of Queens Square.

30. Bridge Street was officially opend in 1863 and the same year saw the construction of the Queens Hotel seen here on the left. In later years the results of General Elections were often announced from the balcony of the hotel. On the right the Lyceum Theatre.

Lyceum Theatre,
Newport, Mon.

31. Built in 1856 by Mr. H.P. Bolt at a cost of between £12-15,000 the Victoria Theatre or Assembly Rooms as it came to be known was described as 'one of the most handsome and commodious buildings not only in Newport but the County of Monmouth'. Amongst the varied entertainment provided there was readings of *A Christmas Carol* by Charles Dickens in 1869. Following a fire in May 1895, it was refurbished and renamed the Lyceum. Its proud boast was *best sound for miles around, greatest comfort to be found*. Included in the list of stars that appeared at the Lyceum was, on 17th April 1905 — for five nights, Ehrich Weiss, better known as Harry Houdini. In 1929 the Lyceum became a cinema until its closure in February 1961. It was later demolished and another cinema (now the Canon) built on the site.

STOW HILL, NEWPORT, MON.

32. A UEC-built number 43 tram makes its way down Stow Hill, about 1910. On the left the junction to Charles Street, in the distance St. Mary's and Wesleyan Churches.

33. Wesleyan Church, Stow Hill. In the early 1880's Methodist Minister W. Gibson made an appeal for funds to 'errect an edifice of architectural design and internal arrangement of a character befitting the position which Methodism ought to occupy in a town of such rapid growth and generally progressive character as Newport'. The church was completed in 1884 at a cost of around £6,000. In 1973, the building changed ownership and today is known as Stow Hill Bethel Temple Pentecostal Church.

STOW HILL NEWPORT MON VW&G. 5551

34. A bird's eye view of Stow Hill, 1905. A tram descends Stow Hill along the single tramway between Clifton Road and Charles Street. On the right the junction of Victoria Place and on the left the Queen Victoria Memorial Almshouses, which were completed in 1903.

35. The Public Benefit Boot Company at the bottom of Stow Hill. Today the site is occupied by the British Gas Wales/Cymru showrooms. On the right, the entrance to Central Chambers.

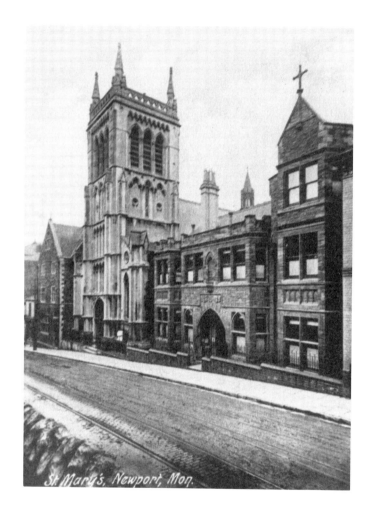

St. Mary's, Newport, Mon.

36. The site on which St. Mary's Church now stands in Stow Hill was formerly occupied by a much smaller catholic chapel. Following the generosity of a Mr. John Jones of Llanarth, who gave the land, the stone for building and a £500 endowment, the first service was conducted there in 1812 when it was reported 'the chapel was crowded and everyone was much pleased'.

St Mary's, Newport, Mon.

37. March 1839 saw the chapel demolished to make way for the construction of a larger church designed by well-known Roman Catholic architect Joseph Scoles. Work progressed swiftly and was only interrupted when the builder, a Mr. Lawrence of Monmouth, and his men were ordered by the Chartist marchers, who were on their way to their fateful confrontation at the Westgate Hotel, to down tools and join them. Scoles' original design included a tower with a spire, but due to a lack of funds a parapet and pinnacles were constructed. St. Mary's was finally completed and consecrated on 11th November 1840.

38. View looking down Charles Street showing the Empire Theatre. Originally known as **The New Theatre**, the Empire which ran two 'houses from 6pm-7.45pm and 8-10pm was one of Newport's favourite entertainment houses for over half a century. At a time when the average weekly wage was around £2 seat prices were: Orchestra Stalls and Dress Circle 1/9 (9 ½p), the Pit 1/- (5p) and the Gods 4d (2p). The last act to play the Empire was piano player Charlie Kunz on Wednesday 7th January 1942. The following day only the burn out shell of the theatre remained, fire having caused extensive damage and its premature closure.

39. Newport Institute for the Blind, Charles Street. The purchase of premises in Newport was made possible through a local appeal, the proceeds of a successful Flag Day which raised £146 and a grant from a local benefactor. Formally opened by Mrs. C.H. Bailey on 19th December 1918, the Charles Street site provided not only office and workshop space but also a shop window for goods made by local blind people. Extensive Institute premises were later opened at Chepstow Road on 29th September 1929.

St. Woollo's Church. Newport.

40. According to legend the first church on the site of St. Woolos Cathedral was founded by Welsh warrior Gwynllyw ap Glywys, King of South Gwent. Gwynllyw it is said was converted to christianity by Tathan of Caerwent and was told in a dream to search for a white ox with a black spot on its forehead and at the place build a church as an act of penitence. Having located the beast he set about constructing a simple mud and wattle church on the site in the 5th or early 6th century.

Newport St Woolos Church (Pro Cathedral)

41. Once described as 'the most noble building in Newport' the main fabric of the church that stands today dates from the 12th century. It was sacked by Owain Glyndwr in the 15th century and has undergone many changes down the centuries. The imposing tower which can be seen from virtually any vantage point in Newport dates from the 15th century having been constructed by King Henry VII's uncle, Jasper Tudor, Duke of Bedford. On the west face is the headless figure the identity of which is unknown with any certainty. One theory, perhaps the most probable, is that it is the effigy of Jasper himself. Some, however, have claimed it is the figure of the King wantonly mutilated by musket fire from Cromwell's soldiers.

42. The creation of the deocise of Monmouth in 1921 resulted in St. Woolos becoming a pro-cathedral and further elevation in its status was gained in 1949 when it became a full cathedral. St. Woolos is unique in Wales by having a peal of thirteen bells, the last of which was added in 1988, the same year that exterior floodlighting of the Cathedral was installed.

43. It is probable that a market house in some form has occupied the site in High Street since the sixteenth century. Then there also stood a whipping post and stocks in which 'many were the pugnacious and evildisposed who obtained a temporary lodgement therein, to the great amusement of the spectators'. This market house was demolished in 1793 and a new building built by the Duke of Beaufort in 1817. Following the purchase of land and market rights from the Duke for £16,500 in March 1885 and adjoining property for £8,500, Newport Council accepted a £13,000 tender from Newport builder John Linton for the construction of a new general market building. An early example of a large span cast-iron framed building, it was completed and opened on 1st May 1889.

Newport. *Market Hall.*

44. An interior view of Newport General Market showing the upper gallery. Taken around 1930 when it seems business, particularly on central aisle fresh fruit and vegetable stalls, was booming.

45. Shotts wholesale and retail provisionist, Newport General Market about 1930. Proprietor Alfred Shott, a senior member of the Newport Market Tennants Association, commenced trading in the market in 1922. At the time the photograph was taken 'delicious streaky bacon' was selling at 6d (2 1/2p) per pound.

46. Shotts Stall, Newport General Market. Note the prices, salmon 5d (2p) per tin, pure butter 1/- (5p) per lb, new tomatoes 7 1/2d (3p) per tin, currants, raisins and sultanas 6d (2 1/2p) per lb and the banner which proudly proclaims 'THIS IS SHOTTS'.

47. For most of the nineteenth century fire fighting duties in Newport were performed by the local police force. In 1884, following a public meeting, a fire brigade of twenty volunteer firemen was formed. A public subscription to cover the cost of uniforms and equipment was opened to which the local council contributed £50. The first fire station was situated in Dock Street and a steam fire engine was acquired in 1885. The arrival of the twentieth century saw the appointment of the first professional fireman and in 1912 the Newport brigade purchased its first motor fire engine.

WESTGATE SQUARE AND TOWN HALL, NEWPORT.

48. Westgate Square and Town Hall about 1907. On the left the Town Hall clock tower, once a well-known landmark, now demolished. In the centre the five-storey Westgate Hotel, rebuilt in 1884/1886, which was the scene of the Chartist Riots of 1839. To the left Stow Hill.

The Waking City, Commercial Street.

49. The Waking City, Commercial Street 1906. Although often referred to as a city Newport has in fact never attained that status. On the bottom right hand corner can be seen Wildings, which was situated on the corner of Llanarth Street.

50. Commercial Street looking towards Westgate Square. On the left Reynolds department store, in the distant right the Town Hall clock tower and building. Designed by architects T.M. Lockwood and E.A. Landsdowne and constructed by John Linton at a cost of £35,000, it was officially opened by Mayor C. Lyne on 24th August 1885.

51. Westgate Square about 1908. On the right, on the corner of Skinner Street, is seen the music shop of Newman and Sons. In the centre, the National Provincial Bank of England, and the number 19 tram en-route to Corporation Road. To the left the familiar ornate cast-iron entrance canopy of the Westgate Hotel.

52. Commercial Street by night about 1906: a post-card manufacturers attempt at a dramatic night scene showing the illuminated shops, number 10 tram and in the distance the Town Hall clock face.

53. Commercial Street about 1910. On the left the Old Bush Hotel, built in 1827. On the right, situated on the corner of Austin Friars, Thomas and Shackell piano warehouse, 'agents for Estey Organs'.

54. The Parrot Hotel situated on the corner of Charles Street was a meeting place for John Frost and his fellow Chartist conspirators. Constructed in 1814, the hotel was rebuilt and renamed the Talbot Hotel in 1885. The site was occupied by F.W. Woolworth until the late 1980's when the store was demolished. Three smaller retail units are currently under construction on the site.

Snowballing Park Sq.

55. Winter fun in Newport. Snowballing in Park Square 1905. On the left is the People's Park.

Statue of Sir Charles Morgan, Bart.,
People's Park, Newport.

56. One of the earliest designated parks in Newport, the People's Park in Park Square was laid out between 1840 and 1860 on land owned by the Morgan family. The park gardens houses the bronze statue of Newport benefactor Sir Charles Morgan Bart. Originally sited in High Street in 1848 the statue was moved to its present site in 1860. In 1988 improvements to the park including repair works to the statue at a cost of £15,000 were approved by Newport Council.

57. St. Paul's Church, Commercial Street. Designed by architect Sir Digby Wyatt, the foundation stone of the church was laid on 19th September 1835 and St. Paul's was consecrated on 3rd November of the following year by Reverend Edward Copleston, Lord Bishop of Llandaff. The freehold site and financial support were given by Sir Charles Morgan, Bart. The church is unusual in having a mock entrance onto Commercial Street. The flight of steps and arches indicate a main entrance when in reality this is situated at the rear. Due to recently discovered structural problems the future of St. Paul's remains uncertain.

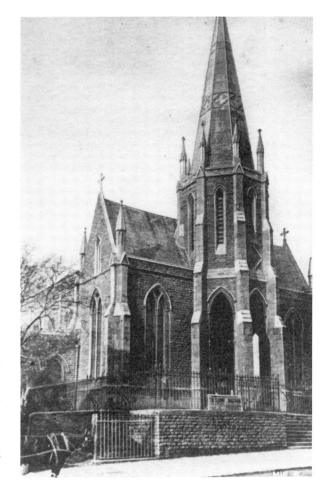

Commercial Street, Newport, Mon.

58. Commercial Street at the junction of Cardiff Road. On the left Thomas' bakery and the spire of St. Paul's Church. On the right the William IV public house, affectionately known as the 'King Billy', which was completed in 1835.

59. *There's not much going on at Newport* − an example of a humorous Newport card, no doubt regarded as 'one for the gentlemen'. Dating from around 1920 it must have then been considered a little daring.

NEWPORT CASTLE, NEWPORT.

TO NEWPORT

I have had so much on my shoulders since I've been in Newport, that I get no chance to write letters, so postcards must do.

60. *I have had so much on my shoulders since I've been in Newport* – the best of both worlds, a humorous card which also featured a local view of Newport Castle.

61. *Greetings From Newport* – another 'one for the gentlemen' from around the same time. It features no less than fifty-seven lovely ladies.

Newport New Hospital

62. The history of health care in Newport dates back to 1839, when a Dispensary was opened in Llanarth Street and relocated in 1843 to a site in Great Dock Street. Six years later, following an outbreak of cholera, 274 patients were treated in one month and twenty-eight deaths recorded in one week. In 1860, the dispensary was again moved to larger premises on Stow Hill. Eventually the need for a larger infirmary became evident and Lord Tredegar's generosity resulted in a gift to the town of three acres of land known as Kings Hill Fields, on Cardiff Road. Following fund raising in the town the foundation stone of the new hospital was laid on 2nd August 1897.

COUNTY HOSPITAL. NEWPORT.

63. The County Hospital 1905. The four ward hospital was opened by Lord Tredegar on 5th August 1901. In July 1913, following representations by Dr. Garrod Thomas, the chairman of the directors, Royal approval for the hospital to be named The Royal Gwent Hospital was granted.

64. Rutland Place, 1906. In the background can be seen the County Hospital, later known as The Royal Gwent Hospital, which had been completed some five years earlier.

65. The number 12 tram on the level crossing at the junction of Cardiff Road and Commercial Road. Prior to 1810 the land where Commercial Road stands was uninhabited low lying marshland – 'At Pill no houses were there found, For it was all rich meadow ground...' Yet so rapid did development of Pillgwenlly become, by 1848 fears were being expressed that the prosperity of the area would detract from the rest of Newport.

COMMERCIAL RD. NEWPORT.

66. Built in 1812, and a familiar landmark before it was demolished in 1963, the Salutation Inn occupied a site on the junction of Cardiff Road and Commercial Road. Around 1840 from the inn for a distance of half a mile there was not a single house on either side of 'Pill Road' as Commercial Road was then known.

67. Commercial Road about 1906. In 1843, it was described as 'extremely dangerous, pits and ravines existed of so dangerous nature that no-one could venture out without serious risk and not a single lamp existed in the whole neighbourhood'. The situation in the area had improved little by 1851, when it was reported that Ruperra Street and New Market Street contained pools of water deep enough for a child to drown.

Entrance to Alexandra Dock showing Waterloo Hotel and Post Office, Newport, Mon.

68. Alexandra Road. In the distance the entrance to Alexandra Dock. On the left can be seen the Waterloo Hotel, built in the nineteenth century by William Moore, which in recent times was briefly renamed Gatsbys before again reverting to its original name. On the left the Alexandra Dock Post and Telegraph Office.

Newport.

Alexandra, N. Dock.

69. Following the granting of Royal Assent to the 'Newport Dock Bill' in 1835, construction of the first dock in Newport began. The first sod was cut by Mayor John Owen and the work undertaken by Rennie, Logan & Company completed at a cost of £200,000 in October 1842.

Alexandra Dock, Newport, Mon.

70. A further extension to the Dock was required and completed in 1858. Soon the increasing trade during the nineteenth century necessitated the construction of the North Dock, which cost £500,000, took seven years to complete and was finally opened on 12th April 1875.

71. The year 1907 saw the completion of the South Dock and only two years later further expansion and widening of the new dock complex commenced. By July, excavation of the new lock to a depth of 50 feet was complete and construction of timbering for the two hundred foot lock wall trenches had almost been completed by the seventy-nine strong workforce.

72. At 5.20 pm on 2nd July 1909, disaster struck when as a result of heavy rainfall during the previous month, the west wing wall trench collapsed. Immediately news of the calamity spread and fears were expressed for the forty-six men who had been working at the bottom of the trench. Five hundred men laboured under difficult conditions in an effort to reach the men trapped benath tons of debris.

73. Amongst the brave rescue workers was a fifteen year old 'South Wales Argus' newsboy, Tom Lewis of Wallis Street. Tom, known affectionately as 'Toya', risked his life amongst the shattered timbers in an effort to save the trapped workmen. Recognition of his heroic efforts came when he was awarded the Albert Medal, presented to him by the King at Buckingham Palace in December the same year. The people of Newport also showed their appreciation of the bravery of the boy hero by contributing to a public subscription which raised several hundred pounds.

TRANSPORTER BRIDGE, NEWPORT.

74. The most dominant feature of the Newport skyline, the Transporter Bridge was described by Lord Tredegar as 'a wonderful and magnificent structure'. Construction work commenced in 1902 and the bridge was opened to the public at 3.30 pm on 12th September 1904.

Transporter Bridge, Newport Mon.

75. During the first four days of operation, 43,000 fares were collected, although Newportonians were a little more reluctant about the ardous climb up and across the 242 foot walkway. When deciding to fix a charge for the journey, one councillor commented: 'It is worth 6d to climb over the top and the council should pay people to do so!'

TRANSPORTER CAR   NEWPORT MON

76. The Transporter is one of only four such bridges built in the U.K. of which only two survive, the other being on Teesside. The joint engineers of the Newport bridge were R.H. Haynes, Borough Engineer, and Frenchman F. Arnodin of Château-neuf-sur-Loire. The cost of the project was £98,000.

77. The Newport bridge has a span of 645 feet and the supporting towers are 242 feet high. The moveable platform which is propelled by two 35 horsepower electric motors housed in a motor house on the east bank has a carrying capacity of six vehicles and 100 passengers.

78. In 1985 the bridge described as 'the standing logo of Newport − the sight local people first look for when returning home' was closed. Repairs costing an estimated £1.5m were required to make it operational again. Calls were made by some to demolish it but public opinion was strongly against this. Because of the apparently insolvable problem it presented the Transporter came to be referred to as 'the bridge of sighs'. However, in 1988 renewed civic pride in the bridge resulted in it being lit up with 1,500 bulbs at a cost of £20.000.

79. Situated between Belle Vue Lane, Cardiff Road and Waterloo Road, Belle Vue Park came about following a gift from Lord Tredegar to the people of Newport of twenty-three acres of land. The site was formerly known as 'Round Table Field' because legend states it to be a meeting place of King Arthur and his knights. The first sod was cut in 1892 and the park was formally opened by Mayor Frederick Phillips on 8th September 1894 at a cost of £19,000.

Fountain at Belle Vue Park   Newport

80. A prize of fifty guineas was awarded to Mr. Thomas Mawson for the best landscape plan for the park. To help alleviate local unemployment the Tea Room was erected in 1910 and in addition to this the park was able to boast a bandstand, a fountain and a miniature zoo.

BELLE VUE PARK.
NEWPORT, MON.

81. The park was the site of Ancient Bardic Gorsedd ceremony of the 1897 Welsh National Eisteddfod.
Performed 'in the face of the Sun − the eye of light' at the 'Sacred Circle' in the park grounds at 9 am on
Tuesday 3rd, Thursday 5th and Friday 6th August, the ceremonies drew large crowds.

82. Newport Intermediate School. Following the Welsh Intermediate Education Act of 1889, the New-port Education Committee met in 1894 to discuss a proposal for a new school. A design from Newport architect Mr. Benjamin Lawrence was accepted and a tender for £7,750 building costs from a Mr. E.H. Read approved. The completed school was opened to eighty boys on 4th May 1896, with a formal opening ceremony by Albert Spicer M.P. on 22nd October the same year. Fees were £9 per annum or £3 per term inclusive of stationery but not books, instruments or music. An extra fee of two guineas per term was charged for instrumental music, singing and painting, and one guinea per term for dancing. In 1920, the school was renamed Newport High School.

83. In March 1911, Colonel Clifford Phillips, Commanding Officer of the 4th Welsh Brigade RFA, addressed the senior boys of the Newport Intermediate School. Following this address a battery of the Newport Royal Artillery Cadets was formed at the school. Their first drill took place on 12th April the same year, with inspection and recognition following soon afterwards. The cadets' uniform of blue tunic, trousers and pill-box hat was replaced soon after with more practicable khaki kit.

Llanthewy Road, Newport, Mon.

M.J.R.8.
1950.

84. Llanthewy Road 1908. In the distance the familiar landmark of St. Mark's Church built 1874. Further up on the left from where this photograph was taken is Llanthewy Road Baptist Church which was completed in 1904.

85. Gold Tops from Godfrey Road 1910. On the right is Devon Place. The familiar landmark of St. Mark's Church dominates the skyline. Always regarded as one of the more opulent areas of Newport, a house offered for rent in 1900 for £25 a year was described as being 'two minutes from the railway station, with three reception rooms, four bedrooms, hot and cold bath, a large garden and greenhouse complete with three vines'.

St. Marke Church   Newport

86. St. Mark's Church, Gold Tops, 1905. In February 1874, four hundred residents from the Gold Tops and surrounding areas were invited to take tea at the Town Hall in the presence of their first Vicar, Reverend T.L. Lister. Six months later the Early English Perpendicular style church constructed of stone from Lord Tredegar's quarry was opened for the first time.

87. Ice skating at Allt-yr-yn, winter 1907. '... the most beautiful part of Newport is the green country called Allt-yr-yn which has a clear canal coming down lock by lock, with Twm-Barlwm in the distance.' (W.H. Davies, Newport's 'Supertramp' Poet, 1918.)

Newport. On the Canal.

88. Following an Act of Parliament in 1792, work began on the construction of the Monmouthshire Canal to serve the needs of the ironmasters of Blaenavon, Nantyglo, Ebbw Vale and Sirhowy by carrying coal and iron cargoes to Newport. Made up of Eastern and Western 'arms' the venture was undertaken by Thomas Dadford Junior using only pick and shovel labour at an original estimated cost of £108,476 13s 9d.

On the Canal, Newport (Mon.).

89. The eastern arm ran 11 miles from Newport to Pontypool rising 435 feet through 41 locks and was constructed in 1796. Completed some two years later the western arm covered a similar distance from Newport to Crumlin and rose 358 feet through 32 locks. The final cost of the venture far exceeded the original estimate and was put at in excess of £220,000.

90. On the canal about 1909. As well as providing passage for the sixty-four foot long barges the Monmouthshire Canal was in later years to prove a recreational amenity for the people of Newport. With the arrival of the railway the former importance of the canal system diminished and the last working cargo boat passage through Fourteen Locks was made in 1930.

THE CANAL LOCKS AT ALTERYN, NEWPORT.

91. The Crumlin arm of the canal closed in 1948 and the Pontypool arm in 1962. After years of stagnation and decay the most picturesque section of the Crumlin arm at Fourteen Locks near Rogerstone was restored to some of its former glory. Under the joint management of the Newport Borough Council and Gwent County Council the site was developed as a public amenity with the creation of a picnic site and interpretation centre.

92. The arrival of John Lysaught's Iron Works, which in turn brought an influx of Englishmen from the Midlands, saw the commencement of organised football in the town. In 1912, a group of local businessmen and workers from the iron works held a meeting where it was decided to form a professional football association team.

93. Originally named the Newport & Monmouthshire County Association Football Club the chosen club colours were black and amber. This choice it is believed was in recognition of the origins of many of the immigrant iron workers who selected the colours of their home town club Wolverhampton Wanderers.

NEWPORT COUNTY A.F.C. 1923-4   PHOTO BY J E THOMAS NEWPORT

94. In 1919, the club was elected to the Southern League First Division. The following year when this league became the Third Division of the Football League, Newport County as the team was then known, became firmly established. Sadly seventy-seven years after its formation the club went out of existence in 1989. Newport A.F.C. formed the same year now continues the future of football in the town.

95. Newport R.F.C. 1910-1911. The pride of Newport, the 'black and ambers' were formed in 1874 and their first match against Glamorgan at Cardiff in 1875 ended with honours even. The team first played at Shaftesbury Park but in 1877 Viscount Tredegar gave land on the east bank of the Usk which was later to become the hallowed turf of Rodney Parade. Over 100 Welsh internationals have worn the black and amber colours and in 1921 one Newport team was made up entirely of Home Union international players.

96. *You can take it from me* − a humorous Newport card from 1904 featuring a 'black and amber' player perhaps underlines the importance of rugby to the town. Ranked amongst the giants of club rugby sides in the world, Newport can boast victories against all the major international touring teams. Perhaps their finest hour was in 1963 when they inflicted the only defeat of the tour on Wilson Whinerays's All Blacks team from New Zealand.

NEWPORT IRISH RUGBY TEAM, 1920.

Top Row.—Reg. Plummer (Referee), T. Regan (Com.), W. Broad, R. Murphy, D. McCarthy (Com.), W. Casey (Chairman), E. J. Lyons, D. Cashman (Co

2nd Row.—J. Collins, W. Casey (Trainer), C. J. O'Leary (Hon. Sec.), J. P. Casey, H. Huish, J. Lenahan, J. Whitfield, J. Lynch, W. O'Neill,
M. Morrissey (Treas.) J. Caper (Touch Jud;

3rd Row.—W. Cashman, J. Shea, Coun. P. Wright (Mayor), M. Casey (Capt.), Rev. Fr. Hickey, Rev. Fr. Cummings, M. Mahoney.

4th Row.—F. Watkins, W. Shea, F. Collins, M. O'Connell.

97. Newport Irish Rugby Team 1920. Following the potato famine of 1846-1847 over one and a half million Irish left Ireland, many bound for the ports and towns of South Wales. In Newport, in one month alone 1,500 Irish people were admitted to the local poor house. The 1861 census for the town showed hardly a single Newportonian lived in some streets in Pillgwenlly and Baneswell, most dwellings were occupied by Irish immigrants or their descendants. Soon accepted by townsfolk, the Irish thrived in their adopted surroundings and played their part in the local passion for the game of rugby football.

Yachting Pond. Shaftesbury Park, Newport.

98. Sailing boats on the Model Yachting Pond, Shaftesbury Park, which was opened in 1906. The park was once a popular venue for travelling shows and circuses.

99. All Saint's Church, Brynglas Road. Built in 1898, the cost of construction and interior decoration was met in full by the Watts family, coalowners and founders of the mining community of Wattsville. 1991 will see the disappearance of this familiar landmark as structural decay beyond repair has necessitated its demolition.

St Mary's Church. Malpas.

Malpas.

Mountain View.

Malpas.

Craig Park Estate. Malpas.

MALPAS

100. Once a small village on the northerly outskirts of Newport, Malpas became a victim of urban sprawl. This card which dates from around 1930 depicts Graig Park Estate, only one of the large housing estates which were to consign Malpas to a fate of mere suburb of the town. The name Malpas is thought to have originated from the Norman-French *Malo Passu* literally meaning 'bad road'. Some things apparently never change as modern day commuters will testify.

101. Malpas was the site of a small priory of monks established by Winebald de Balun in the twelfth century as a cell of Montacute Priory in Somerset. It was the last monastic house in Gwent to be dissolved in 1539. The present church of St. Mary's, Malpas Road, was constructed on the same site.

102. Clarence Place about 1906. Originally known as 'Clare's Place', Clarence Place awaits the arrival of the Cenotaph on the site of the Tramway Centre seen in the distance. On the left Lovells sweet shop.

103. Clarence Place 1914, on the left Newport Motor Supplies, now the ten floor Clarence House office block. In the centre the number 43 tram approaching Chepstow Road, on the left the then new Technical School, opened on 29th September 1910.

Clarence Place. (1) Newport. MON. 350.

104. Clarence Place 1925. On the left the number 23 Caerleon Road tram passing the Cenotaph which had been completed only two years previously. In the distant right Chepstow Road and Corporation Road. Todays scene is dominated by the modern architecture of the H.M. Inspector of Taxes office block.

105. The Cenotaph, Clarence Place. Designed by C.F. Bates and C. Jones, the construction of the war memorial was undertaken by contractors H. Davis & Sons at a cost of £2,996. Work commenced on 24th February 1923 and the foundation stone was laid by Mayor E. Davies in April the same year. The completed structure was unveiled in June 1923 by Lord Tredegar. Recent years has seen much controversy about resiting the monument at a more suitable location.

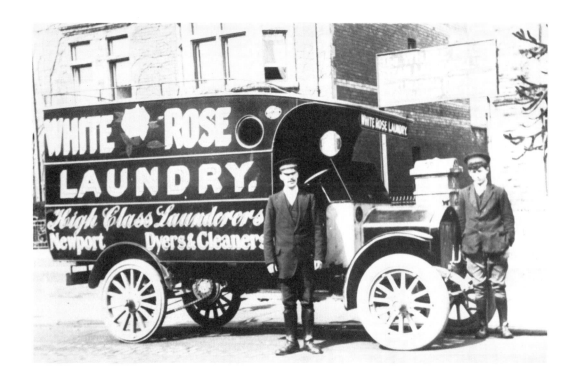

106. The White Rose Laundry of Caerleon Road offered 'The Best in Laundry and Valeting Services' proudly claiming 'A periodic visit to our hygienic dry cleaning works will keep your wearables and soft furnishings smart, fresh and long wearing'. Their vans 'serve in all districts weekly within a twenty mile radius of the town'.

WHIT ROSE LAUNDRY 4TH ANNUAL OUTING SEPT: 1913.

107. The workers of the White Rose 'High Class Launderers' on their 4th annual staff outing to the Wye Valley, September 1913.

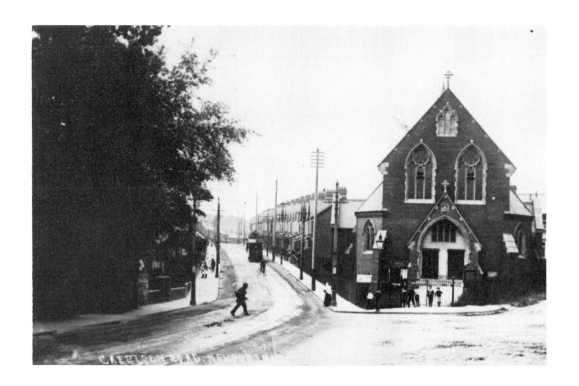

108. Caerleon Road about 1915. In the centre St. Julian's Methodist Church, built 1907, on the left the town-bound tram. To the right is the junction of St. Julian's Avenue. The main Caerleon Road via St. Julian's was first opened in 1825.

109. Caerleon Road 1907, bedecked with flags and bunting to welcome H.R.H. The Prince of Wales to Newport. The Prince was attending the Bath & West of England Show in his capacity as Society President. The Show was held on St. Julian's Hill during the week 3rd-10th June. On the right of the picture the junction to Somerset Road.

110. The arrival of H.R.H. The Prince of Wales in Newport on 6th June 1907. Despite bad weather, crowds lined the route to St. Julian's Hill to welcome the Royal visitor. Here the royal carriage makes it way along Caerleon Road at the junction of Church Road.

111. Off on a trip to the Wye Valley. Riverside neighbours char-à-banc trip to the Wye Valley 1925. Transport to Tintern courtesy of Messrs. W. & A. Pugh.

112. *The Empire Spirit* − 1st. Prize at Durham Road School 1929. The school, built by Newport builders Wm. John Langmaid, was officially opened in 1894.

113. Horrocks Pop Men with their delivery vehicle about 1920. The DW registration plate prefix was in former times commonly associated with Newport vehicles. In the background, on the rail bridge is an advertisement for Colliers, bakers and confectioners, who had premises at Caerleon Road, Commercial Road and Blewitt Street.

114. The class of 1926, Hatherleigh School. Formerly Hatherleigh House, a family home built in the 1850's, the building became Hatherleigh Central School in 1926. After the Second World War its use was primarily as a secondary modern school and in 1967 it became an annexe of St. Julian's Comprehensive School. 1985 saw its closure and it was demolished in 1989 to make way for residential development.

115. Christchurch Road 1904. Housing development at the time had only reached as far as Victoria Manse built in 1897 and seen in the distant centre of the photograph.

The Parish Church, Christchurch, Newport, Mon.
Built about 1000 years. 1558.

116. The earliest reference to Holy Trinity Church, Christchurch, appears to be in the Goldcliff Charters in 1113 where mention is made of 'the church of the Holy Trinity by Caerleon'. Standing on a hilltop overlooking the former Roman fortress, its tower is a prominent landmark for miles around. The church has undergone many changes since the beginning of the twelfth century, not least of all because of three major fires that occurred there in 1859, 1877 and most recently in 1949. Contained within Holy Trinity is the mysterious Colmer Stone, a fourteenth century sepulchral slab which it was once believed had miraculous healing powers. On the right is the fifteenth century priest house.

117. The Cross Hands Hotel, Chepstow Road. The main Chepstow Road via Penhow was first opened in 1817. On the left Spencers stores and the junction of Somerton Road.

Chepstow Road, Newport, Mon.

118. Chepstow Road at the junction of Cedar Road 1905. Prior to 1817 Chepstow Road and the surrounding area were largely an expanse of green fields. The first house constructed between Clarence Place and the railway bridge, was built in 1848 for a Mr. Willmett.

119. Chepstow Road and Caerleon Road about 1911. In the centre the weighbridge machine and office. On the left the number 33 tram making its way towards the town, while the number 27 tram enters Corporation Road.

120. Maindee Square, Chepstow Road, from Speke Street, 1905. Before the 1840's the area scarcely existed and to quote one observer 'with only a few exceptions... there was not a house or building on the land where Maindee and Barnardstown now stand'. On the right is Watkin's provider, suppliers of 'china, glass, earthenware, ironmongery, toys, fancy goods and all manner of other goods'.

CHEPSTOW ROAD, NEWPORT, MON.

121. Maindee Square, about 1905. By 1865 Maindee had grown. Webster's Directory of that year refers to the area as a '...delightful suburb of Newport and contains many elegant residences, chiefly of merchants, professional gentlemen etc., having business at Newport'.

122. By the end of the nineteenth century the increasing population of the Maindee area of the town necessitated the expansion of local public services. In 1898, the Maindee Municipal Buildings on Chepstow Road were completed at a cost of £3,573 and housed a police station, a fire station and a public reading room. The fire station was later closed in 1930 and converted into a public library which, like the police station, still remains today.

123. T.H. Gower draper and millener, 124 Chepstow Road about 1927. Their proud claim was: 'Goods that cannot be beaten for value elsewhere, stock that can satisfy the most exacting demands and lower rents and general expenses enabling prices to be kept at rock bottom!'

Victoria Avenue, Newport, Mon.

M. J. R. B. 7940.

124. During the 'golden years' of postcards, card manufacturers tried to entice people to buy cards by photographing the street in which they lived. This card of Victoria Avenue, also once known as George Hill, from around 1903 is an example.

The Grove, Beechwood Park, Newport

125. Newport is justly proud of its public parks. Perhaps the finest, Beechwood Park, covers twenty-two acres of rising ground on the east side of the town. Situated between Chepstow Road and Christchurch Road, the land was purchased by the council for £11,500 and opened to the public in the summer of 1900. The lower reaches of the park were added in 1924 and officially opened to the public on 22nd October 1925.

BEECHWOOD HOUSE, BEECHWOOD PARK, NEWPORT.

126. Contained within the grounds of Beechwood Park is the former nineteenth century gentleman's residence of Beechwood House. It was formerly owned by George Fothergill, a tobacco manufacturer who built the house on land purchased from The Midland Land Company for £18,000. In 1900, Newport Borough Council purchased it for £11,500. The house was later used as a convalescent home for soldiers wounded in the First World War and in the 1920's as a refreshment centre for park visitors. Recent years has seen the house become a victim of vandals and it has remained boarded up. Plans to demolish it have met with public outcry and have been abandoned. Its fate, as yet to be decided, may be conversion into a nursing home.

127. Corporation Road at the junction of Clarence Place 1920. Completed in 1887, Corporation Road was described as 'a surburban thoroughfare of noble proportions, about two miles long with electric lighting and double lines of electric cars'. On the left the Coliseum Picture Theatre, opened in 1912 and later known to be known as Studio 1 & 2. Also seen on the left are the junctions of St. Vincent Road and Grafton Road.

Corporation Hotel, Newport, Mon.

128. The Corporation Hotel first opened its doors in 1898, just over a decade after the main Corporation Road was officially opened. Here the bar staff and a few regulars of the hotel pose on the corner of Cromwell Road about 1915.

129. One way in which postcard manufacturers increased their sales was to feature a number of views on one card. This composite Newport postcard features a view of the landing stage, Commercial Street, High Street and Newport Castle.

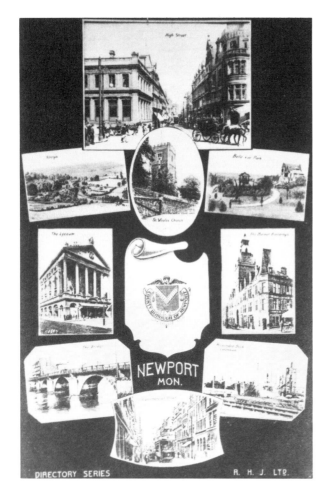

130. Another composite card this time featuring High Street, Alteryn, St. Woolos Church, Belle Vue Park, Lyceum, Market Buildings, Town Bridge, Alexandra Dock Extension and Commercial Street.

131. An interesting composite card which dates from around 1910. Interesting not only for the misspelling of 'NEWPOPT' for Newport, but also for the fact it features Raglan Castle amongst the local views.

Cottage near Ebbw Bridge, Newport, Mon.

132. Thatched cottages at Cardiff Road near Ebbw Bridge 1909. The almost idyllic tranquility is a contrast to the area as it is today.

133. The great Western Railway Disaster, Ebbw Junction. On Saturday 28th September 1907 the 7.40 pm express train from Cardiff was involved in a collision with a coal train. A report from the time stated: 'The destruction, the wreckage of truck and carriage was so great that it is astonishing the roll of killed and wounded was not of a far more formidable character than was absolutely the case.' The driver of the coal train, Thomas Kennett of Cardiff, was killed and thirteen people were injured.

Tredegar House Newport (Mon)

134. The earliest record of a dwelling on the site of Tredegar House appears to date from 1402 when the owner was Llewelyn ap Morgan. The house was rebuilt around 1500 and in 1540 John Leland was moved to comment on it as being 'a very faire place of stone... the elder house of the Morgans of South Wales... caullid Tredegar'. Royal approval of the dwelling was later bestowed by Charles I, who paid a visit on 17th July 1645 after the battle of Naseby. Originally built of stone, the main part of the house was later reconstructed in brick during the period 1664-1672. Amongst the many features of the grounds are a lake constructed around 1790, the splendid iron gates made in 1714 by William and Simon Edney, and a monument to Sir Briggs, the horse that carried Godfrey Morgan into battle at the Charge of The Light Brigade.

The Avenue ... oort, Mon. 14717

135. The ancestral home of the Morgan family for over five
hundred years, Tredegar House was finally sold by John
Morgan, the last of the Morgan family, to the Sisters of
St. Joseph in 1951 for use as a school. In 1974, the house and
90 acres of land were purchased by Newport Borough Council and after extensive restoration and repair it was opened as
a tourist attraction. Today Tredegar House is described as
'one of the most interesting and mysterious Charles II
houses in the whole of Britain'.

136. Newport benefactor Godfrey Charles Morgan, perhaps the best known of the Morgan family for his generosity and exploits in the Charge of the Light Brigade at Balaclava. Born at Ruperra Castle in 1831, Viscount Tredegar's wealth was legendary. His personal wealth in 1908 was put at £11m, his daily income £1,000 and his annual donations to charity exceeding £40,000. His estates in three Welsh counties were believed to exceed 40,000 acres. He became the first Honourary Freeman of the Borough of Newport at a ceremony held at the Great Central Hall, Commercial Street, on 9th June 1909. He died in 1913 and was buried at Bassaleg Parish Church.

137. Cardiff Road 1904. A picturesque rural scene that with the opening of the highway on Tuesday 22nd June 1812 and subsequent ceaseless urban expansion has long since disappeared.

Newport Usk Lighthouse.

138. West Usk Lighthouse, St. Brides. Built to a unique design by James Walker in 1821 for Trinity House, the West Usk Lighthouse was decommissioned in 1922 and sold the following year for use as a private dwelling. It remained occupied until 1930 but then fell into disrepair. It was again occupied in 1967 and in the late 1980's sold for £80,000 for conversion into a guest house.

LIGHTHOUSE SWIMMING POOL, NEWPORT, MON. (2)   G.2021.

139. Bathing at the Lighthouse about 1930. At the turn of the century the Lighthouse was regarded as a popular local resort for Newportonians. Often neighbourhood char-à-banc trips were arranged to Lighthouse Beach for a breath of sea air. In addition to the delights of a putting green, fish and chip shop, coconut shies and children's roundabouts, an added attraction in the 1930's was an open-air swimming pool.

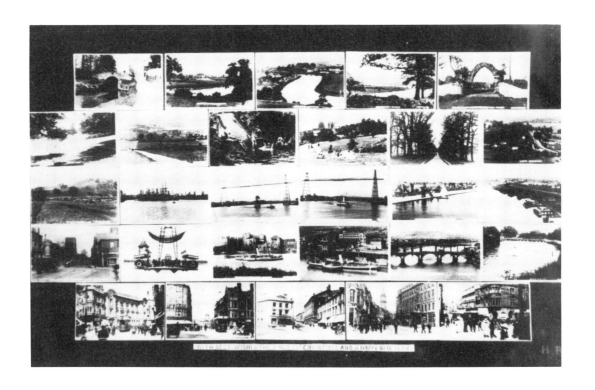

140. The ultimate in composite cards! It features no less than twenty-eight different views of Newport and still finds room for a seasonal Christmas and New Year message.